Walking on Water is a
place: poems that spea
what it means to live ar
From the remnants of
"twists in the dark," Cheryl Unruh expands our ability to see and hear what's on the edge of our horizons as well as the seemingly simple moments that encapsulate living in "the prairie's open hand." She also sparks this clear-seeing with humor, such as in "Making a List," a collection of to-do lists mixing the mythical and ordinary, psychological and geographical. Memory and the power of storytelling, what lies within and around us, and the simplicity of paying attention sing through these poems of home as both a journey into what makes us wild and an arrival into the essence of life.

~Caryn Mirriam-Goldberg, 2009–13 Kansas Poet Laureate and author of *Chasing Weather* (with photographer Stephen Locke)

The hallmark of Cheryl Unruh's prose has always been its lyricism. Admirers of her essays and columns—which is to say, anybody who has read them—will be delighted and not at all surprised to learn that she produces wise, witty, painterly poems as well.

~Eric McHenry, 2015–17 Kansas Poet Laureate

Cheryl's new book of poems re-exhibits her keen eye for Kansas life and her heart for Kansas-land and its people, from its coyote "running for home like a kid / late for curfew" to its "cicadas (that) chant evening prayers." The collection also exhibits her wit, revealed in to-do lists that include "Spend only dimes today . . . Restripe the zebras . . . Do not cry at elevator music . . . Blare Jimmy Buffett until the neighbors complain . . . Toss yesterday to the wind." Such is the way of this collection, full of wit and wisdom, as strong as her prose, but with more vivid light, like a thin blue butane flame.

~Kevin Rabas, author of *Songs for My Father*

Cheryl Unruh brings to her poems the same insider's insight and open-eyed sense of wonder that made her essays about Kansas so delightful. "In a scrappy little town / wooden houses have been / left for dead . . ." we read, and we know she has ridden those silent, dusty, rural roads. The lines: "An airplane, / camouflaged by constellations" have us standing beside her, searching the singularly brilliant Milky Way that arches from horizon to horizon across the nighttime Kansas prairie. "I listen in the dark, / the rain filling a place / I didn't know was empty," she writes, and you find that Cheryl's words work just that way for you.

~Roy Beckemeyer, author of *Music I Once Could Dance To*

Walking on Water

poems
by
Cheryl
Unruh

For my brother, Leon,
who, in my mind, has always walked on water

Meadowlark (an imprint of Chasing Tigers Press)
Meadowlark-books.com
Emporia, Kansas

Copyright © 2017 Cheryl Unruh
cherylunruh.com

Cover and interior photos by Dave Leiker
prairiedust.net

All rights reserved.

ISBN: 1544632495

Library of Congress Control Number. 2017937835

Walking on Water

poems by Cheryl Unruh

A MEADOWLARK BOOK

contents

this land of ours

Walking on Water 3
11PM 4
Morning Coyote 5
After Vacation 6
Wild Horizon 7
On the Kansas Turnpike 8
As Above, So Below 9
Advance Guards 10
In the Flint Hills 11

making a list

To-Do List No. 1 15
To-Do List No. 2 16
To-Do List No. 3 17
To-Do List No. 4 18
To-Do List No. 5 19
To-Do List No. 6 20
To-Do List No. 7 21
To-Do List No. 8 22
To-Do List No. 9 23
To-Do List: Space Mission 24
To-Do List: Winter Beach Party 25
To-Do List: Christmas Prep 26
To-Do List: Acquire Holy Man 27
To-Do List No. 10 28
To-Do List No. 11 29
To-Do List No. 12 30
To-Do List: Writing 31

i

borderline

Souvenir 35
Girl, 14 36
Sunlight 37
Pearl Street 38
Homeless Woman on Clark Street 39
Skin 40
Gulp 41
No Waiting 42
Losing Control 43
Wayfaring Mailman 44
Highway 45
Fear 46
Postcard 47
Light It 48

watching for signs

Playing Possum 51
Sometimes We Cry 52
Friday Night at the Jail 53
The Plot 54
The End 55
The Brave 56
Biopsy 57
Slow-Moving Dreams 58
Thunderstorm Warning 59
Christmas Eve 60
Battles 61
We Knelt 62
A Sign 63
Graduation Day 64
Seventeen Minutes 65
Pause 66
At the Edge 67
"Cat Devouring Bird" by Picasso 68
Venus 69

as it was

That Summer 73
The Church Road, 1970 74
Before We Got Our First Periods 75
Gravedigger's Daughter 76
On Jackson Street 77
What's an Oma? 78
Home Again 79
An Instant 80
The Whims of Electricity 81
Bonnie 82
Mommy 83
The God of My Childhood 84

as the world turns

October Freeze 87
December 4 88
December 7 89
Saturday Storm 90
Patience 91
Winter Kill 92
Snowfall 93
Blowing Leaves 94
Sunday Morning on the Porch 95
April 16 96
May 23 97
Rain 98

About the Photographs 99
Acknowledgments 101
Publication Credits 102
About the Author 103

iii

this land of ours

Walking on Water

When he was young,
my brother, his blond head
bent toward the earth,
searched for sharks' teeth
and gold-gray rocks embossed with fossils.

Sea turtles and sharks
once swam the ocean of Kansas,
leaving their stories in books of stone.

I never really thought till now
of walking on the ocean floor, water
way above my head. Yet as I breathe,
the land billows and I drift
with the undulating sod.

Above the knotted grass,
a summer sky reflects the phantom sea,
where white clouds roll like waves,
haunting an invisible shore.

11PM

Across the street, a lopsided elm
leaps like a buffalo toward
the North Star. Light is gone.
Shape replaces color. An airplane,
camouflaged by constellations,
is blinking, blinking, blinking.
Cicadas chant evening prayers,
"Whee-o, whee-o, whee-o."
A freight train slows to a canter
through town, whistles "wo-woooo"
at every crossing.
Cat beside me on the porch step,
fireflies surround us,
blinking, blinking, blinking.
The planet twists in the dark,
but night never sleeps.

Morning Coyote

Ahead of me, a coyote
crosses the highway.
It's 7:45AM, full daylight. He sprints
over the pavement, down into
the ditch and then up. I'm
far enough away that I'm unable
to see how he gets through
the barbed-wire fence, whether
he slips under or over the bottom wire.
He charges through the green pasture,
glancing neither left nor right,
running for home like a kid
late for curfew.

After Vacation

A congregation of cattle
gossip in the pasture,
their brown eyes unblinking
as I pause along the gravel road.
The meadow sways
with scrappy wildflowers.
Cottonwood trees stand
like fathers, keeping watch
over a thin, rock-bottomed stream.
Last week, in land piled
higher than sky, in canyons
that drenched me with laughing water,
I stood, drinking the sparkling air,
held safely by the cupped palm of rugged peaks.
Still, the mountains cannot call
me home, cannot claim to own me,
cannot embrace me
like the prairie's open hand.

Wild Horizon
Inspired by Wild Horizon,
oil painting by Anna Patricia Keller

There's a rugged line in the west today,
a brown-black row of clouds that hovers,
curling into itself like waves with white caps
on a windy sea. The horizon rises toward
the north, follows a choppy slope of land.

This turbulent sky churns with fate,
pulls itself over the pale and innocent earth.
Brush strokes slide down the
canvas of land, a hint of
late summer's ochre
tucked away to the side.

We live this wild horizon—
it's as familiar to us as our own front door,
a line that keeps us company as the days roll on.
Some afternoons we ride this trail
into a storm of destruction—
but clouds also send rain
for the crops
for the rivers
for us.

Past this reckless horizon,
beyond these painted-on clouds,
waits the welcome blue sky of home.
We linger on the front porch
and watch the afternoon turn into
evening, and evening turn into stars.

On the Kansas Turnpike

In the southwestern sky, the sun wrestles its way out
from behind a skiff of clouds. The low-riding winter sun
lights these afternoon clouds from below for just a moment
and a ray of light shoots across the Flint Hills, sets aglow
the raw umber grassland and reflects off the silver side
of an 18-wheeler bending the curve in front of me.

I drive the Kansas Turnpike today, a four-lane
highway that slashes diagonally across
the eastern third of the state, Oklahoma to Missouri.

I-35 counts its miles from Laredo, Texas,
to Duluth, Minnesota, a long stripe
of roadway through the Heart of America. 1,569.06 miles.

I've driven our section of pavement for decades,
Emporia to Kansas City and Emporia to Wichita.
Thirty years ago, a now-gone sign posted southbound
out of Emporia read: "Enjoy scenic Flint Hills next 31 miles."
William Least Heat-Moon mentioned that sign in his book
PrairyErth and he quoted an actor from New York who said,
"I kind of like a place where the scenery
has to be called to your attention."

We locals don't need that sign, for we are in continual awe
of these rolling hills. On each trip, we watch the light play
over rounded earth, we note shifting colors that the months
and the seasons bring. Unlike most highways in Kansas this
road curves and it winds through a vacant and treeless prairie.
We can see for miles across the soft hills,
across this land that we call home.

As Above, So Below

Clouds will not budge this week.
They are stationary, no movement,
no breath. It's as if the sky
has been painted on. Gray, a flat gray
with no sheen, no shine,
no reflection. Just the gray of an
empty tunnel, a Tuesday gray,
a gray of grief. Years after
you left, here we are, still in
mourning, looking out the window—
but now we are able to see
what has been left behind.
Rain falls, a mist really.
It turns to snow. Small bits, then
heavy wet flakes. Without sunlight,
the flakes are tiny shadows
of sadness falling from the sky.

Advance Guards

A blue-sky morning
surrendered early to weepy
clouds. Wednesday drizzled
all day long, until dusk set in.
Wet leaves crept into the
house on the bottom of shoes
as if they were secret messages
sent by those held hostage
by winter. Arctic cold
becomes an army occupation
camped out in the yard around us.
We lock the door of our fortress,
stoke the fire,
feast on stew and cornbread,
sleep under heavy quilts.

In the Flint Hills

Under a faultless blue sky
the wind slows to nothing
this close to dusk. White rocks
litter the Flint Hills, scattered
with no pattern as if flung
from above.

In the middle of the world,
holding two ends of decision,
neither one right, I let
the darkness fall around me
as the last wash of light fades
on the horizon. I've been here
before, lost, on these grassy hills
where the open sky reads every thought,
where the empty land
keeps vigil with the soul.

making a list

To-Do List No. 1

Decide: church or state

Hoard optimism

Act like a very tall city

Sort through regrets

Hold the silence

Remove nitrites from bacon

Fill rain buckets

Recreate the sound of the spaceship

Plunge into the abyss

To-Do List No. 2

Relocate grief

Worry about nothing

Quiet the voices

Lift the sky

Break the spell

Be a long shot

Unplan my life

Deploy humor

Cling to the old rugged cross

To-Do List No. 3

Pay the gravity bill

Gather intelligence

Vacuum the magic carpet

Put SWAT phone number on speed dial

Write and submit a new book for the Bible

Begin hero's journey

Make a to-do list

Wait on karma

Brew up a new batch of resentment

Vote for Pedro

Cheryl Unruh

To-Do List No. 4

Cancel guilt trip

Have second thoughts

Buy a vowel (Not Y!)

Mail a boat to China

Loiter in the post office

Cross the River Jordan

Swim in the Sea of Galilee

Perform miracles

Pour a glass of wine

Pass go

Collect $200

To-Do List No. 5

Forgive childhood

Practice yoga

Practice hygiene

Practice medicine

Get a second opinion

Have exact change

Spend only dimes today

Sew a pair (or one) pajama(s)

Sow wheat

So what

To-Do List No. 6

Release hostages

Bust ghosts

Pacify the baby

Sink to a new low

Acquire disdain

Confess sins

Climb every mountain

Ford every stream

Renegotiate climate change

Swallow pride

Flirt with a Hell's Angel

Reject tyranny

To-Do List No. 7

Restripe the zebras

Do a primal scream

And a zen howl

Compare the two

Separate sound from silence

Pray for the Milky Way's aging stars

Purchase a cult

Photograph a vampire in its natural habitat
(not at the mall this time)

Hand out beige ribbons for victims of circumstance

Incorporate a small town

Become its mayor

Repeat solemn vowels

To-Do List No. 8

Measure sadness

Photograph the darkest hour

Sell despair on e-Bay

Nap

Apply for tenderness

Practice non-violence

Regain control of the millennium

Multiply infinity by 27

Prep for Big Hair Friday

Extend Happy Hour

Laugh ass off

Deny everything

To-Do List No. 9

Breathe (approx. 20,000 times today)

Construct privacy fence around Acre of Secrets

Accept the Five Stages of Grief

Sweep up old tears

Arrive

Converse with silence

Fold chairs

Squander laughter

Live on a prayer

Elude sleep

Do not cry at elevator music

To-Do List: Space Mission

Refuse Tang

Say hello to Major Tom

Plan galaxy-hopping daytrips

Moon Uranus

Redeem Pluto

Lose weightlessness

Stay tethered to craft

Pack long johns (the ones with the trap door)

Bring extra water (remember how thirsty ham makes you)

Think of clever "one small step" jokes to entertain fellow astronauts

Remember North Star = North

To-Do List: Winter Beach Party

Send out invitations

Purchase blender, limes

Locate swimsuit and flip-flops

Set out Band-Aids

Fill living room with sand

Jack up thermostat to 90

Render frozen concoction

Blare Jimmy Buffet until neighbors complain

Fall asleep in the sand

Swear off tequila

Decide: Was it or was it not my fault?

To-Do List: Christmas Prep

Pre-sing the carols

Wrap the stockings

Clean the chim-chiminey

Expose Santa

Jingle the bells

Dash through the snow

Explain the X in X-mas

Give noodles as gifts (it'll be a surprise!)

~~Be naughty~~

Be nice

To-Do List: Acquire Holy Man

Kidnap a Holy Man. Gently.

Settle him into guest room

Serve him coffee. Or tea. His choice.

Hem his robe

Wash his feet

Ask him about loneliness

About suffering

Obsess about grace

Om everything

Breathe. A lot.

Forgive others, self

Forgive everything that has ever happened

Become One (or Zero?)

Bow to Holy Man

Release Holy Man

To-Do List No. 10

Toss yesterday into the wind

Doubt your existence

Burn your reputation

Exit your wound

Leave the house

Tear up the map

Chase omens

Encourage thunderstorms

Stream sunshine on laptop

Marry the sky

To-Do List No. 11

Create a coincidence

Lower the horizon

Apologize to the pilot

Quit being the worst-case scenario

Spy on the blue house

Reminder: Walls exist for a reason

Create outrageous silence

Pretend you're at sea

Borrow Florida for a week

Become a storm of Light

To-Do List No. 12

Forgive your birth

Forget your story

Erase your identity

Burn the past

Start over (PRN)

Revive your soul

Dream wildly

Live as if you have nothing to lose

Fall in love with life

To-Do List: Writing

Take your characters home for Thanksgiving Dinner

Order strange new words from an online source

Collect random conversations; eavesdrop madly

Soak consonants overnight in salt water

Bake poetry in a 9" x 13" pan, 3 hours, 325 degrees

Ghostwrite short stories at the spooky cemetery in the woods

Braid sentences into girls' hair on the beach (with permission)

Create a pen name (Paper Mate? Uniball?)

Think of a fresh/novel/non-cliche way to say "The End"

borderline

Souvenir

Take me back to that night,
back to the river with its
sleek stones for skipping across the water,
summer trees reaching bank to bank
and me, a teenager then,
sitting on the sandbar
beneath someone else's stars.
I did not belong there that night,
not for a moment,
but still I slipped a smooth river rock
into the front pocket
of my jeans
and carried it home.

Girl, 14

In a scrappy little town,
wooden houses have been
left for dead. The town has a post office
and a bar. Churches have gone
out of business. A car engine
hangs on a thick chain in an
open garage. The man standing
next to it stares at us as we drive by.
In houses, windows are covered with sheets,
or with American flags, blinds drawn
on every window
on every single house along these
streets of dirt and gravel.
A wooden teeter-totter in the park
has nothing left to give except for
splinters, its paint and play
long gone. A teenage girl in jean shorts
walks at the side of the street. Her
long brown hair lifts with each step.
As she turns to look at us,
strangers in her town, her eyes
seem to plead: Take me
with you. Get me out of here.

Sunlight

You stand
against the background of sky,
today a springtime blue.
Golden sunlight
sparkles in your hair.
That ray of sun,
sent to Earth,
raced through the galaxy
at the speed of light.
It landed here.
It landed on you.

Pearl Street

Her old hand with
bent fingers and purple veins
grabbed her ragged skirt,
lifting it to music that only
she could hear.
Her feet knew the way,
twirling on the downtown sidewalk
as if she owned the place.
In her eyes there was something
brighter than the shadows of this world.
Crazy, some whispered as they passed,
but how do we know for sure
who is lost
and who is found?

Homeless Woman on Clark Street

Her face nearly hidden
by wind-tangled hair,
she scrunched
against a storefront and
reached into me with a
predator's eye.
A paper cup shook
in her hand,
rattling its coins,
as she shoved it toward me,
a toll-booth arm denying
passage. I walked on and then
from behind came her
guttural hiss, the sound of a
serpent ready to strike.

Skin

Skin. It barely covers her,
thin as Saran Wrap.
One mistake with a needle
and she's a goner.
One tiny tear in her pearlescent
shawl and she'll come undone,
her veins popping loose,
the corpuscles. Oh man, the corpuscles.

Age spots are the only bit of
skin you cannot see through; there's
not even a wisp of hair on her
arms to keep her warm.
She must be freezing.

She sleeps in her chair,
chin falls against
pink housedress,
white hair wild like fire.

At lunchtime, she sits with the others,
parallel parked. Wheelchair tires
rub against the hallway wall.
They are all
waiting to be chosen,
waiting to be taken.

Gulp

Your anger
is a
stone
that I swallowed.
It
scratched
my
throat
and lodged
in my
chest
like an
aspirin
stuck sideways,
undissolving.

No Waiting

Fayetteville, Arkansas.
An electronic billboard
along I-49 advises:

"ER wait: 0 minutes."

If you're going to
have an emergency,
now is the time.

Losing Control

Downhill
hairpin curves
clenching the seat
she looked at him
driving
blank eyes
staring ahead
her bones shook
inside her legs
screams blared inside
her head
he sped up
tires screeched on the
cliff-edged
curves
she imagined
herself in the car
tumbling
end over end
and him
standing
on the roadway
thumbing a ride

Wayfaring Mailman

I watch for the mailman
who lingers elsewhere
with bag of letters, French-blue
shorts, black socks to the knees.

Maybe he's sunning in Bermuda,
lounging on a sandy beach,
his bag of letters as a pillow.
He steals glances at the softer-than-sand
skin of women's bellies, women's legs,
while waves break at the water-firm edge
of the ocean.

Perhaps he took the letter
addressed to me and threw it
to the ocean in a bottle that now
bounces endlessly on the white-topped
waves, unable to reach my landlocked
mailbox thousands of miles away.

Highway

I left words
scattered on the
four-lane
among the white
painted lines
that separate
me and you.
Between the lines
are spaces - - - -
the silence
I should
have said.

Fear

Underground,
my voice rumbles
like a sky filled with
purple clouds
and I tremble,
afraid the voice
will crack open
the earth
and people will see
inside my thinking brain,
see the fear spiral
in my DNA,
so much a part of me
that only death
will kill it.

Postcard

No name signed,
but I knew
it must be he
who was in Wyoming
this time of year.

He wrote little—
"The long hot August
reminds me of you."

Seven years since
our August, that summer
of anger, not passion.

Why couldn't he
remember April?

Light It

When we abandon the bold yellows,
the reds: crimson and scarlet
When we abandon the fearlessness
of our own fire, and we duck into the shadows
When we abandon the pulse,
the energy, the power that surges
with our very being, we are
denying life itself from taking hold,
we are withholding oxygen
from our cells
We are here to succeed,
to excel, here to shine like the sun
with all of the hot white light
that we can produce

Do not hide
Do not be afraid
Do not back down
Go—
Go into the world, ignite
your passion, your fury
Fire is your birthright

Strike the match

watching for signs

Playing Possum

While driving on Sixth Street,
I saw a cat lying
in an eastbound lane.
Hit. Dead.
A collar.

Someone in town will cry tonight.
It's been me before, crying.
It'll be me again sometime, I'm sure.

Trying to blind my brain,
like I often do when I see
cats or dogs dead on the highway,
I mutter, "It's a possum. It's a possum."

And isn't that what we do
every single day? We try to find ways
to keep our hearts from breaking.

Sometimes We Cry

On the city's main street, wind blows things
up and out of the gutter, half litter, half leaves.
It's winter now, January. Sitting in the coffee shop
I hear "Sometimes We Cry." Van Morrison's voice
scrapes the inside of my skin as it always does.
We have a past, he and I, this song and I.
I played it over and over one October morning,
years ago, as I drove toward a funeral. The windshield
wipers put me in a trance, rain blurred the road,
Morrison broke my heart.
Today, looking out the window, I watch the wind
rearrange the world. I listen to the music without
tears, but the gray sky could drop rain at any minute,
and this saxophone solo is nothing but old sorrow,
a weight around my neck.

Friday Night at the Jail

I scribbled words onto a piece of scratch paper,
words that rhymed with *light*.
The radio frequencies were silent,
the phones were not ringing.
Dispatch in the sheriff's office
was unusually quiet for a Friday night.
On the other side of the cream-colored
cinder block walls, the jailer made his
evening rounds, handing out meds,
heavy metal doors
slamming shut behind him.
A state trooper walked in,
taking a break,
killing time.
He asked, "What are you doing?"
"Writing a poem," I said.
He shrugged, "Yeah, I'm bored, too."

Cheryl Unruh

The Plot

The underworld awaits her.
Beneath the ground, others pace in anticipation,
as shovels dig six feet into the earth.
Spades bisect tough tree roots,
leaving scooped scars in the grave walls,
a growing mound of dirt on the grass nearby.

In the kitchen underworld, church ladies
spoon coffee grounds into tanks of
stainless steel and wonder who will join them.

They wait underground, casket lowered,
damp earth replaced, flowers laid,
tears wiped away, cars driven back to the
homes of the living.

Bent ladies, gray hair tinted and curled,
smile to welcome the descended/ascended.

She arrives in her favorite dress, lavender,
as starched and stiff as she is.
The waiting rush toward her—
her friends and family
greet the fallen,
the risen.
She smiles. She had hoped it would be like this.

The End

Death
was quicker
than he expected.
Cold.
Dark.
Alone.

Where was the light?
The tunnel?
He had thought

death would end
his fears.

Now what?

The Brave

Here we are—
the troubled, the triumphant,
the disabled, the distraught.
We are the brave, the anxious,
the warriors, the worried.
We once were great—and now—
we do not know what we are.
In our uneven faces, our defensive eyes,
our tense shoulders, our stories lie.

And here we are on this green earth, gathered
at a picnic table on a June evening so fine
that even the mosquitoes have left us alone.

Some days we eat scrambled eggs for breakfast,
we answer the phone,
and yet we stand alone in the grocery store
unable to make a decision about peanut butter.
Because life is just that hard sometimes.
On those days, tears burn the inside of our eyelids.

We are not as fine as we once were, age has seen to that,
but we are also so much more. Sometimes we catch a glimpse
of the unseen world and we see through this earthly illusion
with god-like clarity, knowing that everything is perfect,
and exactly as it should be.

Then we blink, and we forget.

And here we are again, the troubled,
the triumphant, the disabled, the distraught.

Biopsy

His voice was raspy,
his energy dimmed,
no light dancing in his eyes today.
Worry wrinkled his words as he
spoke about a biopsy,
the results of which would take a week.
Or more.

I listened from the sidelines—
this wasn't my conversation.
I was nearby, concentrating on a project,
but still, I should have said something—
a kind word, offered a smile.
I should've said something.

Slow-Moving Dreams

An answer I've sought for years
revealed itself in a dream.
The answer played out in
metaphor, of course,
a bank, a balance sheet
but I knew what the dream meant
the moment I awoke.

Mystics say that everything
we need is already within us.
Where, exactly?
In the heart? The spleen?
Running through blue veins?

I've looked
everywhere . . . for so long.
When the student is ready,
the teacher appears.
I swear, teacher, I was ready
five years ago.
I was ready,
I was ready,
I was ready.

Thunderstorm Warning

Lightning drills a spike
into the ground
white hot
white light
against black night.

A beam from the heavens
in search of a target.
Tributaries of lightning branch off,
release energy.

We ourselves carry
fierce electricity—
emotions needing to
discharge.
Some days, we are the lightning
in search of a target.

We find one.
We strike.

Christmas Eve

When you died,
Christmas sparkled in Douglas fir.
Tiny lights splashed on
shiny bows,
promises wrapped neatly with tape and paper.

We promised you hope,
but you knew far more than we
as your frail fingers struggled to
open our gifts.

We watched you converse
with the next world,
walk the line of death,
one side, then the other,
just a step beyond vision.

Battles

She was a deepening
shade of yellow ochre.
Jaundice.
The liver cancer now
obvious to everyone as
we measured her color daily
against white cotton sheets.
In each moment
she found joy in
her struggle to live.
I betrayed her.
In each moment, I longed
for the death she fought,
envious for the end,
tired of the battle, tired
of the never-ending
need to be something,
anything.
We both lost.

We Knelt

We knelt
encircling
her bed
in silence
we prayed
through the veil
she passed
alone
hearts
were torn
heavy
yet freed
as even in death
her spirit lives
as I looked up
we were no longer
in prayer
we were prayer

A Sign

My own decisions
have failed me repeatedly,
so I often ask the Universe
for a sign, a clear arrow
of direction.
In last night's dream, I rode
a bicycle on a tree-lined
sidewalk, a downtown scene.
Winds picked up, dark thunder started,
then heavy rain.

I looked around—
wasn't sure where
to go with my bike.
An announcer's voice,
warning of the storm,
echoed through the downtown speakers.
"If you're looking for a sign," he said,
"This is it: Go home."

That's all I needed to know.

Graduation Day

I sit on a bench along the
town's main street. Two Harleys
shake the air in front of me
while church bells at the First Methodist
play "God Bless America." A whistle
announces a train from the east, heavy
freight plowing through the city.

Down the street, parked cars wait in front of
the diner where new college graduates
face questions from parents about their futures.
Maybe once we could guess the future,
but now the Earth, perched precariously on
its axis, tilts more every day. Who can
know what lies ahead?

All I know is here and now:
birds sing, a young couple passes by,
a cyclist. A train blares, from the west
this time. When I moved here,
thirty-three years ago, I didn't know
if I would ever feel like I belonged here,
but I love this town now—its heartbeat of
trains, the people on Commercial Street,
the sense of finally, finally
being home.

Seventeen Minutes

7:58AM Left the house, stepped around mud in the driveway
from the storms. 55 degrees. Drove eight blocks, parked
in the farmers market lot. Two cyclists fastened helmets there,
readied themselves for a muddy ride in the hills.

Noticed a new vendor couple. I bought a dozen eggs, $3.
They were delighted, their first time at the market,
I was their very first sale.

Picked up asparagus, $4 a pound from Bob the apple man.
Inquired as to his well-being. Said he had spent a day
with a family member at a Kansas City hospital, was glad
to get home, out of the jumble of humanity and concrete,
to walk on dirt again.

Rand greeted me, "Hello, Miss Cheryl." As we approached
a vendor at the same time, he feared I was after
the sugar cookies that he wanted, but I was not.

Tracy, market manager, had her camera. She looked
for customers to pose with a new painted cut-out
of "American Gothic," which was embellished
with vegetables and the market logo.

Ran into Harold, who had seen my name on the birthday
list at the gym. "Happy birthday," he said.

As I get into the car, I see that the community mural
on the back of Mulready's Pub is coming along nicely—
bright colors, strong design.

8:15AM Walked into the house. Told Dave I bought
purple asparagus. "In honor of Prince?" he asked.

Pause

As soon as
he
understood
the importance
of a well-placed comma,

At the Edge

My friend Dan lives at the edge of the earth,
two blocks from the ocean. If he looks past the
diving gulls and breaking waves, he may see Hawaii
way out there, floating peacefully in the Pacific.

Dan spends his days writing fiction, telling the story of
Rolf and Loretta, the German POW and the Mennonite farm girl,
two seemingly different people thrown together during the
last world war.

Figs grow on a tree in Dan's tiny courtyard by the sea.
When the figs pile up, as they do in late summer, he fills jars
with fig jam. A friend sometimes invites Dan over to pick all the
lemons and oranges that he can carry home. I cannot imagine,
as a Kansas kid, trees that dangle with citrus.

From my landlocked home in the center of the continent,
I write to tell Dan about the house-rattling thunderstorm that
woke me this morning, tell him about the essays I'm writing that
describe what "home" means to me.

And from this place, at the edge of the world,
where sand dollars and empty shells wash ashore,
where salt and parrots hang in the air,
where lemons grow on trees as if they belong there,
in his little home by the sea, Dan turns figs into jam,
he turns words into stories.

"Cat Devouring Bird" by Picasso

It's easy to feel sorry
for the bird caught in the jaws
of our husky feline.

The cat wears its stripes like warpaint,
teeth bared, tearing flesh.

But this is simply nature in action,
the turn of the world.
Sometimes birds get away,
sometimes it is otherwise.

Venus

Venus rests in the
curve of the moon this evening.
Mars hangs nearby,
a striking red planet against
midnight sky
lit by a thousand stars.

From my bed, I cannot
see the heavens,
but I am comforted by the steadiness
of the planets,
the stars, the moon.

Tonight I will
fall asleep
safe and secure
between two earthly beings,
one that is snoring,
one that is purring.
To me, it's the same happy sound.

as it was

That Summer

In the decade before I was born, the girls were named
Betty or Beverly or Mary Lou, and their hair was flipped up
and their skirts were poodles.

When I was young, it was Sunday and it was Easter,
and it was the '60s and I wore a new dress that my mother
had hemmed the night before. Made of polyester, a fabric
that couldn't and wouldn't wrinkle even if the dog laid on it
for a year. Not that she did. (The dog.) Or would.
There were Easter egg hunts with eggshells that cracked
like windshield glass and the blue dye had seeped into
the slimy egg white, but the yolk was still good—if you liked yolk.

Soon, it was later . . . and we are now well past the bellbottoms
and the senior pictures and college and weddings and I guess
we're all grown up now. But I've not let loose
of those summer mornings of warm blue sky, and shorts, and Keds,
of bikes and friends, their hair glowing like halos
in the late June sun. We had cookies on the porch and then
we dared each other to jump from a high tree branch
onto the thick unmown grass near the tennis court.
There were Sunday afternoons that lasted into dark,
after the sun went down at 9PM, when fireflies
sprang into action like shooting stars—and everyone
in the small dirt-street town stayed up
well after midnight that summer.

The Church Road, 1970

We dangled our scrawny legs
from the concrete bridge,
the town's drainage ditch below us,
the bottom of which was laden with muddy silt,
hidden frogs, empty beer cans,
and who knows what else.
Some of that smelly silt was on our shoes,
and was flicked away by our swinging legs.
We didn't know, back then, my friend and I,
how innocent we were.
But, you never realize
that you are innocent—do you—
until you're not.

Before We Got Our First Periods

We were curious about Eskimos.
We wanted to be girl detectives.
We wanted to slip our feet into quicksand
to see how strong the suction was;
we were certain we'd be too smart
to get pulled under.

We'd travel the world.
We knew that we could do
anything we wanted to do.
We knew that we could be anything we wanted to be.

Gravedigger's Daughter

Dad, how did it feel
to mark out the plot,
to lay the framework down?
How did it feel to dig up the
first chunk of earth
and to keep going farther down?

Dad, how did it feel
to be digging a grave,
especially one for a friend?
And now that he's dead,
do you think of when
your time on Earth will end?

Was filling a grave any easier,
were there any tears you hid
when dirt clods tossed from your shovel
bounced on the coffin lid?

Dad, I know it was long ago
when you filled those earthen mounds,
but you never said how it felt to you,
digging those holes in the ground.

On Jackson Street

So many ramen noodle meals: beef, oriental, pork.
Ten packs for a dollar in 1977. Kraft Mac and Cheese,
four boxes for a dollar. I didn't have many dollars.
Half-price meals during a shift at McDonald's kept me fed for
two months. One roommate brought home fried chicken
on nights she closed at KFC. And mashed potatoes, biscuits.
We feasted those nights: grease and gravy.

Glenda, our nosy landlord, kept close tabs on us.
She lived upstairs, but came down to do laundry
(and likely snoop) when we weren't there.
If we were home, she'd yell, "Girls, can I come down?"
The three of us would look at each other,
eyes wide. Susie was the one to say, "Yes,"
because Karla and I couldn't hold our laughter.

A semester, the three of us, in that little basement.
A living room open to the kitchen. A bedroom. A tiny bath.
Karla left in December. Now two of us. College went on,
homework, partying, work, boyfriends. When a ferocious
blizzard shut down the town in February, Susie and I walked
four blocks in knee-deep snow to a restaurant open
on the main drag.

Winter turned to spring. I was 18, turned 19 there.
It was my first apartment away from home.
Nothing better than that.

What's an Oma?

I did not have an Oma or an Opa,
Not a Mimi or a Papa. I had no Nana, no Granny, no Gramps.
Not even a Meemaw.

I was handed the regular-issue grandmas (2) and grandpas (2).
Did I miss out on anything?

My paternal grandparents were German, were not huggy kind
of people, but I was loved, and I was given the chance to see
an axe taken to a chicken's neck, was offered the taste
of cow tongue boiled on the stove. When I was 9,
we cousins played pitch with my liver-spotted grandmother
until 3AM. When we slept over, I was bathed, cooked for,
covered with quilts on winter nights. I was lifted and spun
in the air by a strong-armed grandfather.

If we could choose, would we choose what we had?
Or would we choose something and someone totally different?

Before coming to Earth, we each draw from a hat
names written on paper, like a fortune tucked into a
folded cookie. Congratulations, baby human child,
You get an Oma! And an Opa!
A Mimi and a Papa! (Warranty not included.)

Do not complain, little one, or grown-up, if that's what you
are now, because for some the fortune is left blank,
and those without are left to only imagine.

Home Again

Rear tires hum a
moonless lullaby
to the stars
while we speed
68 in a 55.

Front-seat voices blur
into a blanket wrapped
warm around me
while stars stretch thin white lines,
constellations of flannel circus animals.

The window cools my head,
its vibrations in theta
override my decades on this earth,
and I dream, knowing that
when fog voices end, Dad
will lift me out of backseat sleep
and cradle me into sweet white clouds.

Cheryl Unruh

An Instant

You buried
your pain
once and for all.

In an instant.

A bullet
left no doubt
as we stood there,
summer sun on the
graveyard ground.

The Whims of Electricity

With its cream-colored face,
the electrical outlet frowned.
Secured in the wall next to the family dinner table,
six inches from my 3-year-old ear,
I kept an eye on that outlet at every meal.
Someone, likely my brother, told me to never
toss water into the outlet because it would
shock me. So I was careful with my drinks.
Spilled milk frightened me—what if a drop of it
splashed into the outlet?
I always wondered how the electricity
would know, if two or more were gathered, exactly
who the water-thrower or milk-spiller was?
To whom would it lash out?
Would it zap my brother if he were the cause?
Or would it strike me, the one whose right ear was a
mere six inches from the socket?

Spring thunderstorms remind me of that
outlet. Clouds, purple with anger, breed
lightning. Veins of electricity shoot up the night,
aiming to kill, looking for someone to blame.
Would lightning hit a guilty party?
Or would it strike an innocent woman who just
happened to be near?

Bonnie

It was the slant
of her nose
that caught his eye.

In the black-and-white photo,
she was the one looking left
while everyone else
smiled at the photographer.

He paused, the photo in his hand.
He wished he'd known her then,
still hope in her eyes
in those years
before he was born.

Mommy

The child's cry
in the night,
"I want my Mommy,"
doesn't go away
at 4, at 8, at 35.
Pillow
clenched to my chest
when the sun sets and
the world of night
gets heavy.
The only comfort,
my lifelong friend,
holds me without knowing,
catches my tears
from a thousand miles away
whispers words
drowned out by whimpers.
She hums a lullaby,
brushes back hair
stuck to my tear-wet face
and rocks me back to sleep.

The God of My Childhood

He wore a blue suit, white shirt, maroon tie,
a Lions Club pin on his lapel.
His voice droned on,
pleading the law of the day:
"Love those who hate you."

I watched the second hand. It didn't move.
In the pews, Amy and I played
Connect the Dots in the margins of bulletins,
whispering, giggling, till we were told to hush,
then warned again with the "I mean it" eye.

Windows pushed up on the summer day.
Light blew in, a welcome change from the
milky-green stained glass of winter.
We cooled ourselves with cardboard fans
donated by Beckwith Mortuary,
the place you go to when you die.

God is there in the mortuary,
to deliver or condemn. By deeds we live,
by deeds we die. Love those who hate you.
I mean it.

as the world turns

October Freeze

Tonight, geese are flying south
in the freezing rain,
their honking caught
between cloud cover and earth.

My body is tense, guarding against the cold.
It is as stiff as the trees which are frozen in place
with ice dangling from limbs like
Christmas ornaments.

Autumn left without saying goodbye,
forced out of town like the geese.

The furnace runs endlessly,
my body not yet adjusted
to the solstice not yet arrived.

December 4

I woke to full sunshine,
dancing skies of blue.

Two hours later,
thick clouds lower the ceiling.
Rain is falling,
reminding me that December
carries the weight of winter:
the coming snow and
sleet and wind chill,
the daily litany of
coats and scarves and gloves,
the shivering skin,
the slow-moving blood.
We've been here before,
dozens of times.
We are like planted
crops and the calendar
circles around us,
circles around us.

Come what may.

December 7

The first snow of winter
comes down in exclamation marks.

It's snowing! Everyone shouts.
They point out the window,
or if outdoors, they reach to
catch the delicate carvings of sky
that melt on warm hands.

Smiles, all around, watching
flakes fall, bigger flakes
than we remembered them to be.

New. White. Clean.

We remember being six—and the
mittens and stocking caps, forts,
snow angels and snowballs. We
remember hands and feet, red and chapped,
burning from the cold. We remember
sleds and flying downhill
and not knowing what would stop us.
Sometimes it was a tree.

Summer gives us lightning bugs;
winter gives us snow.

Saturday Storm

The common snowflake, the
tiniest invention of winter,
fills the city with silence today.
The temperature drops,
bitter cold settling in. White sky,
white roofs, white street,
white lawn. I say white as if it's
true, ignoring the nuance of light,
ignoring the depth of palette as seen by an
artist who nudges blues and purples,
yellows and pinks into her smear of
titanium white. Outside my window
a swirl of flakes is caught in the tunnel of
wind. The flakes ride helplessly
beneath the eave of the neighbor's
house until each flake
lands somewhere, presumably.
The season's first accumulation
brings a hush to the world,
a quiet library in which to read a
thick winter's novel, undisturbed.

Patience

December is a marching band
that is marking time, going nowhere.
Patience is the daily lesson of winter,
so we wait in this season, the one with its
own songbook. Page 28.
Let it snow. Snow. Snow. Let it.

In this, the season of guilt, winter
scolds us from behind its velvet
curtain. Placed in timeout, we sit
with our beads, move fingers
stone to stone, we bow,
chant our penance:
Forgive me this, forgive me that.
Hail. Grace. Mother of God.
Let it go. Go. Go. Let it.

As we resolve and absolve our sins
with beads, sleet falls, ice.
Cold air whiskers in through
a crack in the door.
We've nowhere to go.
Mother of patience, mother of forgiveness,
I am not a believer in this snow,
snow, snow. Let it go.

Winter Kill

Winter killed her
as sure as a knife in the back.

It could've been the
body-stiffening cold
that sucked the life from her
as it weaseled into the house
under the door and through
frost-laden windows.

But I know it was the gloom of gray
that pressed down to the earth so low
it smothered her like a bulky feather pillow
clamped over her face, her arms
free and flailing up to the sky,
reaching for the negligent sun.

Snowfall

White
flakes
float down
from the heavens,
glittering
in the purple glow
of a streetlight.

Gently,
ever so gently,
snowflakes light
on bare branches
which still mourn the
loss of their leaves.

A sapling shivers
alone,
silent,
and prays
for the coming of spring.

Blowing Leaves

My neighbor shut off her leaf-blower to shout
across the street. "Do the trash men come tomorrow?"
It was December 27, and the sanitation schedule had
shifted to allow for holidays. "Yes," I yelled back,
then crossed the street to visit.

"That wind,"
she said of the 45 m.p.h. Christmas Day gusts,
"blew the leaves off her tree,"
pointing to the stubborn oak next door,
"and onto my yard, so now I'm trying to get rid of them."

I, too, get blown leaves from a neighbor's trees.
But I've found that if we are patient,
the Kansas wind will eventually send most of them on
to the next house, then the next, and the next.

And I thought about other things that come into
our lives like those leaves, unbidden, the things that float through:
conversations, people, nods and smiles, sunrises, new moons,
old moons, friendships and true loves. So much flows through
us in one small lifetime. If you sit still and close your eyes now,
you can watch that parade in your mind—the people,
the opportunities, the moments—and see them roll by.
Each one of us gets to choose:
the moments and the people that we hang onto,
and the ones that we let pass through.

Sunday Morning on the Porch

With leafless trees, February owns more sky
than June ever will. These gray trees are the bare
bones of winter, all branch and all bark.

Meanwhile, crispy leftover leaves from November
tumble head-first, somersaulting like a juiced-up
four-year-old girl, rolling, rolling, rolling.
Our lawn is a sorry shade of brown, a low-cut carpet,
waiting for something better to come along,
waiting for spring rains, for longer days.

There is no Sunday silence here. A breeze fills the
void between bird chatter and dog conversations, between
dueling motorcycles riding down the city street and
trucks whining on the interstate a mile away.

Last autumn, the neighbor to the north sold her house
and moved, taking down the wind chimes that had hung
on her porch for years. Their deep and hollow tones
always called me to presence.

As I lean against my porch pillar, rays of sunlight
settle into each of a thousand pores on my face and warmth
races through those tiny tunnels in my skin.
The golden sunlight burrows into my veins. Today,
it's the sun that calls me to presence. I close my eyes.
I need nothing more.

April 16

O wind, you're such a narcissist—
on and on and on you blast,
a tiresome soliloquy of
run-on sentences,
reckless words that set the
prairie afire.

Please leave this scarred and
wind-scraped land.
Take your empty chatter on up to
Nebraska; you're headed
that way anyway.
Slam the door if you must.
Just go.

May 23

Sometimes thunder
kicks down the door
like a teenage boy
filled with angst,
reckless, loud,
a demolition derby in the sky.

But today, thunder is an
old man, hesitant,
lurching through the clouds,
the pain of age
pulling at his bones.

Rain

All day, rain has
held to the clouds,
the sky turning from gray
to purple to purple-blue
and back to gray again.
A soft wind, the breath
of spring rain, pushes the yellow kitchen
curtains into the room.
Now, as dusk falls,
so does the rain,
darkening the sidewalks,
the street. As cars drive by
the sound of wet tires
splashes in through the open windows.
I listen in the dark,
the rain filling a place
I didn't know was empty.

Dave Leiker's photographs
are available at prairiedust.net.

acknowledgments

Much love and appreciation goes to my husband Dave Leiker for his continuous support of my creative endeavors. The stunning photographs on the cover and interior of this book are Dave's work. I am ever so grateful to Tracy Million Simmons, who has done a marvelous job of editing and designing this book and its cover. My brother Leon Unruh also provided invaluable editing and commentary. Thank you, Leon. My heartfelt thanks go to Kevin Rabas, Caryn Mirriam-Goldberg, Eric McHenry, Roy Beckemeyer, and Dan Markowitz for their feedback on this collection. I am grateful to the Emporia Writers Group for their writerly companionship—and a toast goes to Mulready's Pub for providing a great environment for us writers.

"11PM," "After Vacation," and "Rain" first appeared in *The Christian Science Monitor*.

about the author

Cheryl Unruh loves words. And sentences. The flat land of Kansas. Sunshine. And a big blue sky (puffy white clouds are optional). She builds poems, essays, and short stories at a small desk in her home in Emporia, Kansas.

She is the author of two books of essays, *Flyover People: Life on the Ground in a Rectangular State*, a 2011 Kansas Notable Book, and *Waiting on the Sky: More Flyover People Essays*, a 2015 Kansas Notable Book. Cheryl has won awards from the Kansas Press Association and the Kansas Association of Broadcasters. She received the 2016 Kansas' Finest Award from *Kansas! Magazine*.

cherylunruh.com
flyoverpeople@gmail.com

also by Cheryl Unruh

Flyover People: Life on the Ground in a Rectangular State
2011 Kansas Notable Book

Waiting on the Sky: More Flyover People Essays
2015 Kansas Notable Book

Available at
quincypress.com

meadowlarkpoetrypress.com

Meadowlark Books is an independent publisher, born of a desire to produce high-quality books for print and electronic delivery. Our goal is to create a network of support for today's independent author. We provide professional book design services, ensuring that the stories we love and believe in are presented in a manner that enhances rather than detracts from an author's work.

We look forward to developing a collection of books that focus on a Midwest regional appeal, via author and/or topic. We are open to working with authors of fiction, non-fiction, poetry, and mixed media. For more information, please visit us at www.meadowlark-books.com.

Also by Meadowlark

GREEN BIKE

MoonStain — poetry by Ronda Miller

To Leave a Shadow — Michael D. Graves

Songs for my Father — a collection of poems & stories by Kevin Rabas

Books are a way to explore, connect, and discover. Reading gives us the gift of living lives and gaining experiences beyond our own. Publishing books is our way of saying—

> *We love these words,*
> *we want to play a role in preserving them,*
> *and we want to help share them with the world.*

meadowlarkbookstore.com

Made in United States
Troutdale, OR
07/21/2024